I0704604

© 2024

This book of yinzer jokes
and puns belongs to:

____

FOREWORD

Yinz better buckle up for some silly clean jokes and puns – the kind your yinzer dad would be proud of you telling! If you do not understand the jokes, you may need some yinzer training! Go redd up your room before you start telling these dahntahn or anywhere. And remember, these are just jokes and not meant to be an indication of reality in any way.

Have fun n'at!

This book is dedicated to Larry, and his baseball opener joke (one among many dad jokes) that inspired this book.

#1

Pittsburghers drive on the right side of the road until pothole season: then they drive on what's left of the road.

#2

Why do thieves love Pittsburgh sports? Because they love the "Steal"ers…and Pirates.

#3

Why won't the Pittsburgh Pirates drive
on the Yellow Belt?

The road is 'scurvy.

#4

What did the incline worker say about
her job?

"It has its ups and downs."

#5

Why doesn't Allegheny County public works staff ever lose their pants?

Because the roads have six belts.

#6

Why don't they sell bottled drinks at PNC Park?

Because they always lose the opener.

#7

Why couldn't the verbose man find the fountain at the three rivers?

He could never get to the Point.

#8

Why was the Heinz family always the slowest in a race?

They always had to ketchup.

#9

On what day of the week was the
Pittsburgh salad invented?

On a Fry-day.

#10

The Allegheny River is always reliable.
You can bank on it.

#11

Why doesn't the Ohio River like the West End Bridge?

Because the bridge is its arch-enemy.

#12

Where do yinzer authors go dahntahn to write?

Penn Avenue.

#13

Why did Dippy the Dinosaur cross the road?

Because the chicken wasn't around yet.

#14

What is Dippy the Dinosaur's favorite book?

The thesaurus.

#15

Why does Allegheny Cemetery have gates and walls around it?

Because yinzers are dying to get in.

#16

What is the best key to open the Pittsburgh Zoo?

A monkey.

#17

What do you name a baby born in Mount Washington?

Cliff. And you should drop over to say hi.

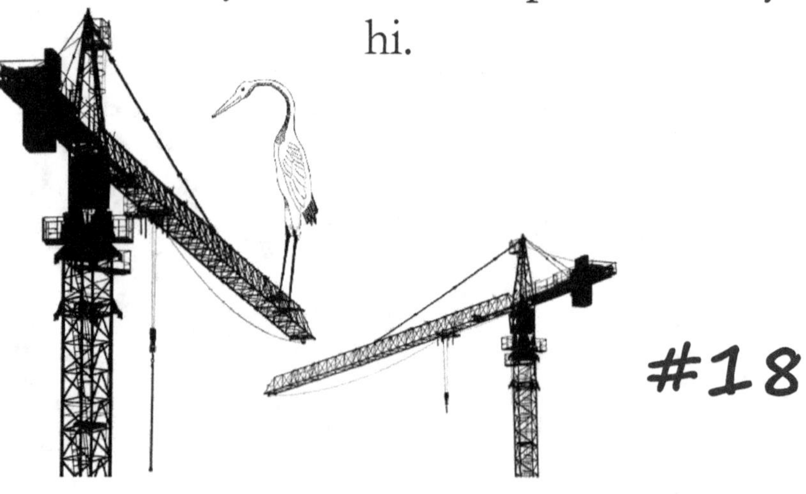

#18

What is the best bird at the National Aviary to work on construction?

The crane.

#19

Why are Pittsburgh squirrels always late
for work?

Traffic is nuts.

#20

What did the construction workers say
when digging out the Fort Pitt Tunnel?
The work was boring.

#21

I didn't want to be obtuse, so I went to Market Square. That's acute joke.

#22

What's the best time to meet at the old Kaufmann's Clock?

6:30 - hands down.

#23

Why are the traffic signals in the Strip District always red?

You'd be red too if you had to change in front of everyone.

#24

Why did the yinzer think the Monongahela River was Jamaican?

Because it was a river Mon.

#25

Pittsburgh bridge engineers have a lot of truss issues.

#26

What vegetable is banned on the Gateway Clipper?

Leeks.

#27

What do the pirates charge for corn on the cob?

A buck-an-ear.

#28

If the county jail prisoners took their own photos, they'd be called cell-fies.

#29

Who are the penguins' favorite team
relative?

Aunt Arctica.

#30

Did you hear the joke about the U.S.
Steel Building's roof?

Never mind, it's over your head.

#31

I was afraid to go to the Andy Warhol Museum. I heard there were lots of sketchy drawings.

#32

How do you have a party at the Carnegie Science Center?

You planet.

#33

Why did the Ohio River listen to the latest pop music?

It was trying to stay current.

#34

How did the Ohio River listen to the latest pop music?

Streaming, obviously.

#35

Why is Grandview Avenue the best
place to forgive someone?

You can overlook everything there.

#36

Why is the Parkway East the best place
for playing music?

You can always count on a good jam.

#37

Someone stole the toilets from the old county jail. Police say they have nothing to go on.

#38

Why can't Pittsburgh see very well?

It only has one "I"

#39

What's it called when a Primanti sammich falls apart?

A slaw-der.

#40

What's the best meal to eat driving the Parkway West?

Brake-fast.

#41

Why are the math professors in Oakland the saddest of all teachers?

They have too many problems to work out.

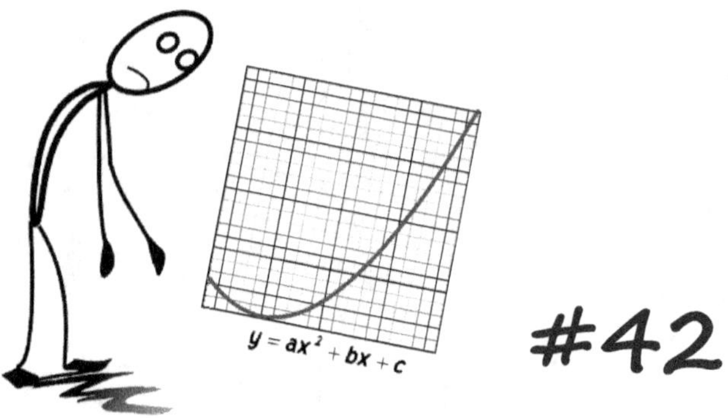

#42

Where do you take an injured French person in Pittsburgh?

If they're grateful, Merci Hospital.

#43

Why don't the Pittsburgh busses run on time?

Because they run on wheels.

#44

Why doesn't the "T" light rail run on time?

Because it runs on electricity.

(You thought I was going to say tracks, didn't you?)

#45

How does the Penguins hockey club
build a team?

Igloos it together.

#46

Why are there so many Nobel Laureate
scientists from Carnegie Mellon
University?

They keep their ion the prize.

#47

Did you hear about the lazy set designer at the Benedum Center who got fired?

He didn't make a scene.

#48

What's a yinzer's favorite dog?

A Pitt Bull.

#49

Why wasn't Fort Pitt made entirely of doors?

Because then it would have been Fort Knocks.

#50

Why do scammers like Point State Park?

They like to be near the con-fluence.

#51

Why are the Pittsburgh rivers so rich?

Because they each have two banks.

#52

Why do Penguins goalies get so rich?

They're great at saving.

#53

How do the flowers at Phipps Conservatory whistle?

Through their tulips.

#54

Why are the plants at Phipps always the best sports fans?

They're always rooting for the home team.

#55

What was Andy Warhol's favorite breakfast?

The Pop Tart. No, actually it was a bowl of surreal.

#56

Why did Andy Warhol give up painting still life art?

It wasn't moving.

#57

My great grandpa lived next door to the inventor the Ferris Wheel – but didn't know him. They ran in different circles.

#58

Yinzers are afraid of speed humps, but they're slowly getting over it.

#59

Why are the hospitals in Oakland the
best place to wait?

They have the most patience.

#60

Why did the restaurant in Deutschtown
have trouble getting customers?

The owner kept telling everyone it was
the "wurst" place.

#61

What are yinzer fishermen's favorite food for dinner?

Pier-ogies.

#62

Why did the police show up at the Lenten Fish Fry?

They heard two fish got battered.

#63

They reconstructed the West End Circle. That made it hard to get around.

#64

Why did the bouncer turn back the yinzer with jumper cables?

He didn't want him starting anything.

#65

Where are you most likely to hurt your Achilles heel in Pittsburgh?

Troy Hill.

#66

Want to hear a joke about Pittsburgh roads and potholes?

Sorry I'm still working on it.

#67

Why didn't the sun go to the University of Pittsburgh?

It already had a million degrees.

#68

What part of Pittsburgh does the sun dislike most?

Shadyside.

#69

Why don't yinzers crush their pop cans
for recycling anymore?

It's soda pressing.

#70

Why do the Steelers love the arcade?

They always play with four quarters.

#71

Why were construction workers struggling to build the Fort Pitt and Fort Duquesne bridges?

They were just trying to make ends meet.

#72

The first Ferris Wheel was made of steel because if it was made of aluminum, it would have been non-Ferris.

#73

What happened when the yinzer fell in love at the steel mill?

Sparks were flying.

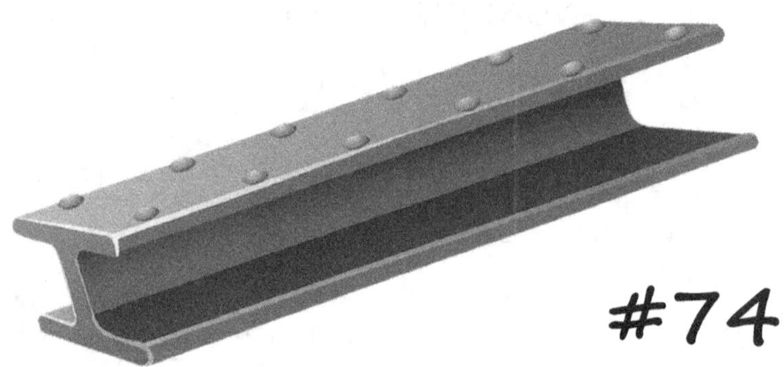

#74

Documentaries about the Pittsburgh steel industry are the best. They are so riveting.

#75

Where is the best place in Pittsburgh to
grow flowers?
Bloomfield.

#76

What language do Pittsburgh bridges
speak?

Span-ish.

#77

The PPG Buildings, made of glass, were difficult to build. In fact, they were quite a pane.

#78

Why did the yinzer kid get arrested for refusing to nap?

He was resisting a rest.

#79

Why do hikers laugh so much in Pittsburgh?

They are hill-areas.

#80

I'd tell you a joke about dippy eggs, but
I don't yolk around.

#81

My hands were cold walking up Fifth Avenue, but worse on Fourth – they were even number.

#82

Why did the yinzer get a job at Breadworks?

They kneaded dough.

#83

Why did yinzers ask Rivers Casino to put cows on its roof?

Because they liked high steaks.

#84

Why do Pittsburghers think they see monsters while driving through the hills?

Must be tunnel vision.

#85

What did suspicious Pittsburgh salad say
to the other Pittsburgh salad?

I've got my fries on you!

#86

Why won't tea go up the inclines?

It was too steep.

#87

I'd marry you at the Strip District produce terminal, but I cantaloupe.

#88

What do dentists do before riding the Thunderbolt at Kennywood?

They brace themselves.

#89

All those Pittsburgh city steps are very suspicious – they're always up to something.

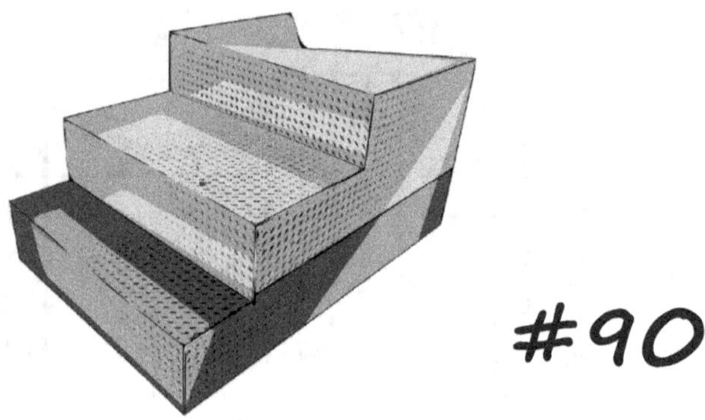

#90

Pittsburgh geology is interesting, but geography is where it's at.

#91

Why is the Pirate Parrot so good at improvising?

He really knows how to wing it.

#92

What kind of grades did the Pirates get in school?

High C's.

#93

The U.S. Steel Building isn't the tallest building in America, but it's up there.

#94

Why aren't more yinzers historians?
There's no future in it.

#95

I asked a parking chair for a loan but it wouldn't support me. It did help my small apartment because as a great space saver.

#96

I got a compliment on my parallel parking dahntahn. Someone left a note that said "PARKING FINE."

#97

Why was the Pittsburgh Symphony percussionist so happy about the broken drum?

You can't beat it.

#98

You should really attend the Picklesburgh festival. It's a big dill.

#99

Why did the chicken cross the road to Sandcastle water park?

To get to the other slide.

#100

One time a jagoff threw milk, cheese, and butter at me.

How dairy.

Thank you!

We hoped you enjoyed these 100 Yinzer Jokes & Puns! Yinz have a great time sharing with your friends n'at.

What were your favorite yinzer jokes?